LORNE HOLDEN

MAKE IT HAPPEN

in

▼

10

Make it Happen! Lorne Holden

Minutes a Day

The Simple, Revolutionary Method for
Getting Things Done

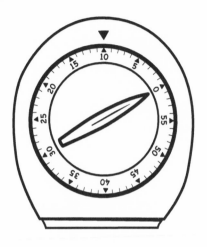

Artwork

Nicole Zaccaria

Design

Danny & Ulana Chapman

Contents

There are no great acts.
There are only small acts,
done with great love.

— Mother Theresa

Introduction

Flower by Flower

You're busy, right?

If you picked up this book, then your answer is yes and we have something in common - not enough time. And perhaps the sense that large things can't be created or conquered because we don't have the big time they require.

I offer a simple solution: make intentional ten minute efforts every day.

This idea was borne out of necessity in my life. During a recent summer, I was still in the labor-intensive phase of raising my young son. I longed to put in a flower garden, but as a single parent with neither partner nor family nearby, time for such endeavors did not exist.

Still, I wanted that garden.

So one day, I bought a six-pack of impatiens and upon returning home, I got out of the car, dug one hole and planted a single flower. Then I went inside to attend to the many things that needed my attention. I left the other flowers in their container at the edge of the grass. And for the rest of the day, I could feel that one flower singing. All day long.

Something had happened: I was back in the flow of possibility. Step by step, flower by flower, and day by day, I created a garden that knocked me out with its beauty. I never spent more than ten minutes on it, because I never had more than ten minutes. Nonetheless, its magnificence was the single most sustaining element of my world that summer. Every day, its beauty soothed and inspired me. I would look down on it from the window above and feel proud, accomplished and ... sane.

Not only was the garden itself incredible, but every time I looked at it, I was reminded that I could make things happen, even with very small amounts of time. The flowers became my cheering squad, encouraging me to remember this new blueprint for action. I no longer felt at the mercy of my situation and the joy I experienced inspired me to apply the technique to other corners of my life.

It was a quiet, daily revolution.

I have deliberately kept this book short, to the point, and delivered in concise chapters that can easily be read in ten minutes or less, so the book will be a first taste of its own fundamental premise. The information begins with the Make it Happen concept and how to get going with it, and then continues with advice and specific suggestions.

The world is full of books and ideas about time management. However, as I have just learned, time cannot truly be managed. We can only ever manage ourselves.

MAKE IT HAPPEN is written to help you do just that: manage yourself - your energies, intentions, and activities. It is a recipe for endeavor, to help you create what you want in a way that is consistently possible and filled with joy.

And in case you are wondering, yes, I wrote this book in ten minutes a day.

The Idea

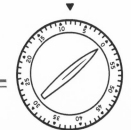

What's Ten Minutes, Anyway?

Think back to the last time you were pulled over by a cop for speeding.

It took forever for the cop to get out of the cruiser and saunter over to you. Then it took you an embarrassing amount of time to find your license and registration, and try to talk your way out of it. Then it took an hour for the cop to go back to his car, look up your statistics and decide whether or not to give you a ticket. Tick. Tick. Tick. And when he eventually got out of his car to walk back over to you with the piece of paper in his hand? An eternity.

In fact, in most situations, that whole scenario wouldn't take much longer than ten minutes. So, if ten minutes can feel that long, it can actually be that long. Which means you can create ten minute blocks of time that offer up that same sense of expansiveness.

What it takes is clarity and intention. Figure out what you want to create or conquer, put your mind to it and work in incremental amounts of time every day. Your actions will quickly bear fruit and amaze you. Seeing the growing results will give you incentive to continue and before long, your project or dream will be consistently blooming forth in measured steps, every day.

It can happen.

Read on.

The Power of Ten

Ten Minutes a Day
is
Seventy Minutes a Week
and
280 Minutes a Month
and
Sixty Hours a Year.

Let me say that again.

Ten minutes a day is sixty hours a year.

Imagine spending sixty hours this year pursuing the experience you have dreamt of for so long, but never felt you had the time for.

Imagine spending sixty hours this year conquering the tasks that you constantly avoid.

Imagine spending sixty hours this year learning a new language, doing yoga, writing a novel, practicing an instrument, singing, or growing your own food or finally, finally cleaning out that cruddy basement or reorganizing those closets. Then, imagine what else you might be doing, having accomplished all of that.

Imagine.

Time Bloom

A powerful thing about approaching a task with Ten Minutes a Day is the way it triggers your involvement. Ten minutes often becomes the portal through which you find your initiative. The timer goes off and you barely notice because you are so happily involved in what you are doing.

There is a mysterious exponential effect that seems to happen. Working with purpose, you climb inside of time and it stretches, blooms. Ten minutes becomes more than ten minutes. Suddenly you have a new ease of inclination and are in the swing of involvement. Tomorrow's ten minutes may grow into more than ten, and you'll be witnessing the impact of your actions every single day.

Always bear in mind that your own
resolution to succeed
is more important that any other one thing.

— Abraham Lincoln

Remember: to work incrementally, day by day, is to work in the way of nature. It is no surprise that growing a garden was the act that taught me the power of this way of working. I would do my ten minutes, and the garden would do its day of growing. Day in and day out. I was in synch with both my desire for the garden and the reality of my time constraints. Nature was in sync with herself. And together, we created a miracle in the front yard that changed my life.

The Time Inside of Time

Once I loved a book so much that I couldn't bear to put it down. When I had to get to an appointment, I put it in my lap in the car and picked it up every time I stopped at a red light. It worked. I read it. There was time that happened then, while I sat at red lights in the car. I call it: The Time Inside of Time. Cracks in the day when time passed unnoticed.

Following this lead, I started keeping reading material next to the stove while I was cooking. The hidden down-time in food preparation became my secret mental getaway. I would seize it.

Another time I needed to paint the small room off my kitchen. I kept a plastic container of paint, a paintbrush wrapped in tin foil (to keep the paint from drying) and a small drop cloth in the corner of the room. And little by little, square foot by square foot, the room got painted. Sometimes I would do something as small as paint one panel of woodwork before I left the house for the day. It was a minuscule act but such gestures moved the project along. It took about ten days but that was far less time than I would have spent standing around wishing the room looked different and doing nothing.

Three obvious places that the Time Inside of Time exists is while we are waiting, commuting, or in the arc of time between commitments. Waiting at the doctor's office. Taking the subway to work. The time between preparing to head out the door in the morning and the moment you actually leave. These are places where small amounts of time could be used to great effect. It isn't necessary to become a maniac, never letting yourself rest. Simply look for the places where time is washing away, and see if you can claim it and use it toward creating/conquering the things you desire.

Where does this kind of time

exist in your life?

How can you grab it?

A New Mindset

Working in the MAKE IT HAPPEN mode requires an essential tinkering with your inner self. You have to dial up your patience and alter your relationship with gratification.

Hard to do and disappointing, yes?

Well, no.

While it's true that you do forfeit the giant, instant variety of gratification, instead you embrace a smaller, daily dose of joy. Every day you may get less done, but you are always in the doing.

Working on a day to day basis, using short amounts of time, you have the knowledge that you are consistently acting on behalf of what you want. The new sense of gratification is immediate, reliable and rewarding. The journey becomes the joy.

Knowing you are only asking ten minutes of yourself will encourage efficiency. Being busy is not necessarily the same as being productive. With the MAKE IT HAPPEN approach, you can take a wide, lazy hour of unfocused energy and turn it into a happily charged and productive ten minutes.

When beginning to work this way, it is important to remember that you are entering into a new relationship with your time and energy. And as in all relationships in life, you want it to be a good one. You want it to make you happy. When I told my neighbor I was getting ready to write this book, she said "Are you really going to force yourself to write for ten minutes every day?" The truth is, I am not a fan of forcing myself to do anything. So my answer was no. But I did end up working for ten minutes nearly every day because I considered the dailiness and the time limit an invitation, rather than an obligation.

It was not long before my project had its own momentum and the initial invitation transformed into a genuine, internal drive, as I loved what I was doing. My energy became self-replenishing as I moved along at a manageable, continually productive pace. As the Tao says, "The softest thing in the world overcomes the hardest thing in the world, as water will wear away rock." Working ten minutes a day allowed me to flow gently forward with my creating. Daily. Happily. The process stayed light and the project got done.

You are holding the proof in your hands.

Remember...

Like attracts like.

So when you put daily energy into things you love and want to do, you naturally attract more of that experience. You find the part of yourself that wants to do all those other things too. You become activated, so your life becomes charged with a greater sense of possibility.

Your experience of this mode of action no longer becomes just about the ten minutes you spend but about who you have become as a result of this form of engagement. You are a success every single day. You are closer to a dream, every single day.

You are no longer the person who has always wanted to learn Italian. You are the person learning Italian. Think of what that self-knowledge would do for how you feel about the rest of your life.

Find a place in yourself that you trust and try trusting it for awhile.

– John Cage, Composer

Make it easy.

Take it easy.

Keep it easy.

The Make it Happen Mantra

3

How To Begin

The Start Sheet

For many, simply starting a new endeavor can be the hardest part. Make this easy on yourself by taking your first ten minutes to brainstorm and dream up your plans with a Start Sheet. If even this feels daunting, remember – you'll only be at Square One once. Then you will be in the swing.

Find a timer and set it for ten minutes. Take a sheet of paper and draw a single line down the middle. Or, if you are going paperless, create a document on the computer and use the clock on the screen as your guide. On the top, left hand side of the page, write the word CREATE to list the dreams and projects you've yearned to make happen. On the top right, write CONQUER to list the tasks you've been avoiding or dread. There are also pages at the back of this book, with the words CREATE and CONQUER on them. Use them if you wish.

Aim to write three to five ideas in each column and then let yourself go. Don't think too much - just start. Pay attention to the first thing that leaps to mind in either category and don't judge what comes up for you. Trust yourself and let your thoughts pour forward.

Keep your statements brief and pro-active. Example: instead of writing "Spend less time on Facebook", write down what you would like to do with that time. Instead of writing, "Edit that idiotic article that Aunt Helen keeps wanting to submit to a magazine" simply write, "Conquer Helen's article." This way, you will already be using your first Ten Minutes in both a positive and economical way. Keep your statements simple. As Steve Jobs famously said : " Simple can be harder than complex: You have to work hard to get your thinking clean to make it simple. But it's worth it in the end because once you get there, you can move mountains."

This is a powerful first gesture in many ways. First, because you'll be hearing from yourself about what you want. Always a good thing! You may find you write things on your Start Sheet that you didn't even know you felt. A long forgotten dream bursting forth? An obligation so dreaded that you've managed to ignore it persistently? It's all information and a beginning.

Making a Start Sheet will also give you a chance to experience how much can be done in ten minutes, as well as possibly giving you a first experience of how the Time Bloom effect can happen. When the timer goes off, invite yourself to quit or keep going according to how you feel.

Here is a sample Start Sheet that I wrote about the things I would like to create and conquer in my life right now.

CREATE	CONQUER
1. Write this Book	1. Write a will
2. Improve my vision	2. Clean out the garage
3. Find five new things for dinner	3. Organize all our toys
4. Learn Spanish	4. Get the family paperwork in order
5. Breathe more fully	5. Back up computer files
6.Write long overdue email to dear friend from whom I've become disconnected	

Note that the final desire landed in both columns because it is both something that I really want to do but also feels weighty because I have put it off for so long.

Next

With your second ten minutes, which can happen immediately (time blooming!) or the next day, your task will be to create goals out of your desires.

Take another piece of paper or make a new document, and again make two columns. Title the left column "WHERE I AM NOW", and the right, "WHERE I WANT TO BE." Go through each point on the Start sheet and state where you are now and where you would like to end up.

WHERE I AM NOW	WHERE I WANT TO BE
I have a smattering of Spanish remembered from high school.	I am fluent in Spanish.

OR

I have no will.	I have completed my will, and given copies to the appropriate parties.

Enough cannot be said about the importance of writing down your goals. Clinical Psychologist Dr. Gail Matthews of California's Dominican University did a study on the impact of writing down one's goals and made the following conclusions:

- The list of goals becomes a written contract to yourself which usually sparks a personal motivation to achieve them.

- Creating the list makes you define clearly

what your goals are. Writing them down encourages you to state what you want in greater detail.

- The list itself frees your mind of perpetually thinking and "remembering" your goals.

- The act of writing down your goals stimulates creativity and motivates you to think about the next step.[1]

As with the Start Sheet, there are pages at the end of the book with space for you to jot down your answers regarding Where You Are Now and Where You Want to Be as well as your Timeframe. Take your next ten minutes to fill these out.

1 Matthews, Gail. October, 2011
http://www.dominican.edu/dominicannews/study-backs-up-strategies-for-achieving-goals

Buddy Up!

A great way to get going and stay motivated is by working with a buddy, or accountability partner. As in every endeavor in life, things are easier and more fun if you have the continual support of someone who is facing a similar challenge. Two people working side by side have more fire in their engines, and can help keep each other focused and on target. The old saying "two minds are better than one" is absolutely true. In fact, two minds can often create a third, collective mind, that is frequently more than the sum of its parts.

What to Do

First, be selective in your choice of buddy. Make sure that you choose someone who will support your efforts unconditionally, hold you to your intentions, and also offer up a hearty laugh whenever possible.

Define a way of working that is both realistic and fun. Want to meet once a week or just talk on the phone? Send a weekly report by email or compare actual notes when you are sitting in the same room? Meet in a coffee shop? Take a walk while you talk and think? Decide what works and then stay fluid with the process. Remember to keep things simple, effective and fun. Your buddy system should stay as light and easy as your own ten minute process every day.

Remember that your buddy is your supporter, not your jailer. And vice versa. When you have a bad week and don't meet your goals, your buddy's job is to understand and help get you back on track, not judge and condemn you. If your buddy responds harshly, get a new buddy.

Another way the two of you can support each other is by creating a Time Swap, where you assist each other in your endeavors. If you are learning Italian, perhaps your buddy can assist you in unravelling verb tenses. If your buddy has an accounting project, maybe you can offer insight. The Swap is different than merely checking in, because you are actually offering your time to your buddy's endeavor while they are returning their energies to you in kind.

I, myself did not have a buddy when I built my garden. What kept me going was the interplay of my own ferocious desire and the daily rewards that kept showing up. Could I have done more if I had had a buddy? Perhaps.

If you don't have a buddy, let this book be one for you. Check back in with it, look at the chapters you find most compelling and dive into the support on the various social media outlets listed in the back.

The key component to having your Buddy system work is acceptance of one another's starting point and complete unconditional support. No shame as you begin, total support as you progress, shared celebration as you finish.

Keep it easy.

Make it Fun.

Time Frame

It is up to you if you want to create a time frame for your project.

Example : Do I want to be fluent in Spanish someday? Or do I want to be fluent in Spanish in three years? It's only ever up to you, but if you do have a time frame, dare to state it. Words are powerful. Words written down are doubly so. As the legendary motivational speaker Paul J. Meyer states: "Writing crystallizes thought and thought produces action."

When I started writing this book, I had a general sense that I wanted to complete it within six months. At the five month mark, it was clear I was nowhere near finished. So I took that original deadline off and simply kept working. A few weeks later, I again felt the need to define a timeline and gave myself a new target: three months away.

I took this new deadline very seriously. I stated it to the creative team working on the book and to everyone else supporting my journey. I held myself to it. I gave working time frames to the designers and artists assisting me (example: "I need this part complete in one week") and they always met their goals. As a result, we stepped up, worked apace and the project was completed on time. There was no harrowing eleventh hour race to the finish. There was simply the satisfaction of a job done well, completed with a paced and steady ease.

Deadlines get results.

Set one if you feel it will help you achieve your goals.

Motivation is what gets you started.
Habit is what keeps you going.

– Jim Rohn, Author

Marking the Time

A great ally in working in the Ten Minutes a Day mode is a timer. The timer does exactly what it is meant to do, mark the ten minutes that you are asking of yourself. It also allows you to immerse yourself in what you are doing without having to worry about noticing or counting where you are. The timer takes responsibility for the time. Let it.

Remember that the timer is a liberator, not a dictator. It is meant to give you that "school's over for the day!" feeling when it rings. And when you hear that bell, you can then decide to knock off immediately or continue what you are doing. You are either finished or immersed and up for more. It is only ever up to you.

Because I work from home, I use a kitchen timer when doing things around the house. If I am working at the computer (writing this book, for example) I simply check the time on the screen as I begin and then only ask myself to do ten minutes.

Remember the mantra:

Make it easy.

Take it easy.

Keep it easy.

We are what we repeatedly do.
Excellence, then, is not an act
but a habit.

– Aristotle

4

Making It Happen

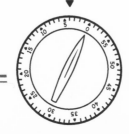

Creating the Little Dream

Little dreams are projects that can be completed in a relatively short amount of time. These endeavors have less emotional load than Big Dreams or Dreaded Obligations, so a Little Dream is a great way to start using the MAKE IT HAPPEN method.

Examples of little dream activities in my life are: helping my son conquer a new task, working on small home improvement projects, and of course, gardening. In moments of extreme resistance or laziness, I remind myself to do the math: ten minutes a day is over an hour a week. And as we know, an hour of focused energy and attention can add up to great things.

Key to making the Little Dream happen is both making it light and keeping it convenient. As with exercise, you will be more inclined to move into an activity if it's easy to get to. When I painted the room described in "The Time Inside of Time", what allowed me to keep going was the fact that the paint and paintbrush were always there, at the ready. If I had had to dig out my tools each time, I would never have gotten the job done.

Start today! Success of your Little Dream Project will be encouraging. And as a result, you may be up to beginning a Big Dream or conquering a Dreaded Task.

Keep it Easy.

Take it Easy.

Go!

Creating the Big Dream

"You mean now?" Yogi Beara once responded, when someone asked him the time.

Yes, now.

Learn a language.

Master an instrument.

Write a screenplay.

Invent a product.

Big dreams often require a lot of time and tremendous dedication. To go after a big dream can feel daunting but there is nothing more powerful that simply beginning. Ten minutes a day can be your toehold to a great start.

"Doing does it!" my Dad would always say. It's true and yet sometimes not so easy.

If your dream is both long held and not yet acted upon, perhaps there something is in the way. It is important to identify what is blocking you before you dive in. Reach for a friend, partner, buddy or therapist for help if you need to.

Consider these ideas:

- Double check to make sure that what you want is indeed what you want. You will have a greater chance of success if you are following a true path.

- Do you feel like you are allowed to go after this goal? It's possible that not having inner permission is what has been holding you back. If not, how can you get to a place of permission?

- Know yourself and your tendencies. If you are a private person, write down your goals in a journal. If you are more social and enjoy interaction, get a Buddy or tell your spouse or friend that you have decided to create something great. Let them hear your words, and hear yourself as well.

- Make sure you have all the support you need.

Remember, ten minutes is a small bite. Your first several ten minute experiences might simply be to ponder what it will feel like to engage in this creation. Your next step might be to create a structured agenda for how the time will play out. You are always your own best expert. Create a structure for how you use this amount of daily time that will give you the best possibility for success. Above all, don't give up.

Enthusiasm is one of the
most powerful engines of success.
When you do a thing,
do it with all your mind.
Put your whole soul to it.
Stamp it with your own personality.
Be active, be energetic,
be enthusiastic and faithful,
and you will accomplish your goal.

– Ralph Waldo Emerson

The Big, Dreaded Obligation

The only way I can describe how to approach a big, dreaded obligation is by describing how I went about one of my own: writing a will.

I was masterful at putting this off for a long time, simply because the whole idea felt too overwhelming and sad. I would remember that I needed to do it, immediately become flooded with sorrow, imagine that the whole process would be agonizing and then become stuck and do nothing. Over and over again. It was only when I realized I could work in tiny steps, taking a bite-sized approach, that the task seemed surmountable.

I began by opening an easy door first. For my first ten minutes, I called a friend and asked her if she had a will and how she went about creating it. This was a great ice breaker, as the gesture felt both easier and less intimidating than if I had initially spoken to a lawyer.

I continued this for several days, contacting people I cared about and trusted, to inquire about their decisions in this weighty matter. For a few of the days, I used my ten minutes simply to think.

Next, I looked into simple online options for creating a will. There are many. When I found a site that felt like the right fit, I took a deep breath and dove in. Again, I kept it simple. On the first day, I completed the mundane portions of the file, relieved that I didn't have to face anything that was emotionally charged. As the days passed and I faced the harder parts of decision making, I stuck to my ten minute time limit and stopped immediately when the timer went off. The Time Bloom effect never happened here. In fact, I experienced the opposite – the time limit felt like my ally and protector. I was able to do ten minutes worth of writing and then save my work and stop. I always stopped and was relieved to do so.

Half way through, I decided to reward myself when I finished. I planned a wonderful evening out with a friend. (See note on this in "Words of Advice.") This had the same galvanizing effect as an accountability partner, because I really wanted that reward and knew I couldn't have it until the job was done.

Ultimately, I completed the job and the relief was immense. The grim task had become manageable only because I didn't have to do very much of it in any one day.

An additional source of support would be working alongside an accountability partner who was doing the very same thing in their own life.

Again, here are the key components that helped me:

- Open an easy door first.

- Find a way in that feels inviting.

- Stay true to the ten minute limit if you need to.

- Trust yourself and trust time.

- Plan something fabulous to do when you are finished.

- Work with an accountability partner if you feel that will help.

Keep it easy.

Always remember:
You're braver than you believe,
stronger than you seem,
and smarter than you think.

– A. A. Milne

That Niggling Thing

This is the annoying little chore that needs to happen. It hums in your consciousness, though not loudly enough to be addressed. You can always put it off. So you do.

Whatever it is, swat that fly! Give it ten minutes of your attention today.

Here's my own example of a small, tedious thing to conquer:

At the end of summer, I can't stand when it becomes necessary to wrap up the summer fans and put them in the basement. Inevitably, the fans are covered with dirt on the inside and need to be pulled apart and cleaned and then wrapped and taken downstairs. Additionally, my inclinations are hampered by the fact that putting the fans away is a clear reminder that yes, summer is really over.

If I expected myself to wash all the fans, wrap them and put them away, I would never do it. The only way I can get myself to do this is by doing things the Ten Minute way.

Here's how I break the task down:

Day One: Take one fan, pull it apart, wash it. Leave it to dry.

Day Two: Wrap that fan and take it to basement.

Day Three: Take second fan, pull it apart, wash it. Leave it to dry.

Day Four: Wrap that fan and take it to the basement.

And so on.

If it sounds simplistic, it is. Thank goodness for that. Because if it weren't for this simple approach, I would spend the whole fall dreading this chore, putting it off and feeling resentful until...the following summer when the fans are still stuck in a corner of the house, now doubly covered in dust. I've actually done that – avoided putting the fans away for an entire winter and spring.

Additionally, this is a ten minute zap of action that I can do before work. So at the end of the week, I've actually succeeded in getting the fans put away and don't have to consider it the chore that I am facing for the weekend. The chore is done. The weekend is free to be what it's really for – fun.

As the wonderful life and business coach John Assaraf says: "Small shifts make a big difference over time."

The best way to predict your future is to create it.

– Anonymous

5

Words of Advice and Support

Time is Elastic –
Slow it to Grow it

Ten Minutes can feel like ten hours if you are really bored or really anxious.

Waiting at the check-out counter, while the cashier-in-training leaves to find his supervisor.

Sitting in a doctor's office, anticipating a medical diagnosis.

Wondering where your teenager is at midnight.

Awaiting the arrival of your one true love at the airport, after they have been delayed at customs.

Waiting for a jury verdict.

The daily routine of caring for an infant.

These are all examples of when the elasticity of time is most apparent.

Time can become an endless ocean if you are moving

slowly.

The lesson: When you slow time, you grow time.

Likewise, the opposite seems to be true.

If you move quickly, time moves with you and moves quickly too.

This is a simple key then:

Slow down

and you will have

more time than you think.

The Antidote to Procrastination

Procrastination is a powerful force in many of our lives. It's easy to put off tasks that feel hard.

The key energetic component to procrastination is resistance. You think of something you need to do and you immediately resist the idea. Then inertia sets in and....

If all that you are asking of yourself is ten minutes, then there is very little to resist. Knowing you only have to engage in a difficult or long-ignored task for a short amount of time, makes the whole concept easier to approach. And as we know from the Time Bloom effect, ten minutes is what pulls you into the flow of engagement and then once you are there, you are there.

If you have a big, dreaded task and you can't get yourself to even begin, consider this: John Perry, Professor of Philosophy at Stanford University, developed an idea he calls the "Theory of Structured Procrastination." The theory holds that procrastinators can be motivated to do important things as long as they are doing them as a way of avoiding something even more important.[2] I find this both hilarious and absolutely true.

We can use Professor Perry's idea to help here.

So, you really, really don't want to clean out the garage, right? That's fine. Would you be willing to clean out the refrigerator? Approaching a smaller and more manageable task might be a way of shifting you into a forward

---

2 Perry, John. November, 2011
http://www.structuredprocrastination.com/

momentum. Once the fridge is clean, and you have the satisfaction of it, you may feel more inclined to tackle the garage.

Believe you can
and you're halfway there.

– Theodore Roosevelt

Identify What is Stopping You

Another way to help yourself get going is to identify what is stopping you. There is usually a niggling kernel of truth that is getting in the way. Can you sleuth it out? Can you solve the dilemma?

Here are some examples:

Scenario One

You absolutely do not want to clean out the garage.

Niggling truth: It's filthy.

Possible solution: Get industrial strength rubber gloves, a simple face mask and some old goggles you can later throw away. If it's the dirt that is really bothering you and you are protected from it, you may be more inclined to dive in.

Scenario Two

You do not want to write the term paper in the class you can't stand anyway.

Niggling truth: You hate everything about this task.

Possible solution: Pull out all the stops. Try implementing the "Divide and Conquer" idea or offer yourself a reward that you really, really want. Coat the experience with every imaginable joy. Create a contest for your social media sites which invites people to offer up the most encouraging words ever spoken. Eat something delicious before you sit down to work. Watch a great movie when you are halfway through. Turn the task into a challenge of how many wonderful, hilarious things you can do while you are writing that will keep you going. Create a list of those things and figure out how to submit the list as a poem somewhere.

Scenario Three

You cannot face clearing out your friend's apartment, who has just passed away.

Obvious truth: It's devastatingly sad.

Possible solution: Define how you can support yourself completely. Not just a little – but completely. Bring in other friends who share your sadness, or alternately, a neutral friend who has no connection to the loss and whose role would be to support you completely. If you have all the emotional scaffolding you need, the practical aspects may not feel so overwhelming. If possible, engage in the process a bit at a time. Offer yourself a reassuring experience to follow each time you face the sad experience. Think of three ways your life feels good to you, write them down and carry the list in your pocket. Pull it out and read it whenever you need to.

The thing to remember is that putting things off usually feels awful. Completing dreaded tasks feels great.

Choose to do the thing that feels great. Do it ten minutes a day- nibbling at it until the task shrinks in size and is finally complete.

Start today.

Do the difficult things while they are easy
and do the great things while they are small.
A journey of a thousand miles
must begin with a single step.

– Lao Tzu

Create a Reason for Completion

The single most powerful motivator for me to clean the house is knowing that people are coming for a visit or a party. I become incredibly effective in short amounts of time and take a higher level of pride in creating beauty than I would if just cleaning for myself.

If you find you need something to motivate your activity, think of ways to create a serious spark.

Some ideas:

Want your house to be cleaner and more organized?
Invite someone over soon for a simple visit.

Want to get that attic finally, truly sorted out?
Consider having a Gang of Ten Party (see Specific Ideas).

If that doesn't feel right, set a date in the future and invite people over for a specific event to be held in the space. If the space is not a good one for a gathering, invite them over anyway and show off the newly cleaned space.

Be realistic about the date and be bold in sending out invitations for a situation that is not yet real.

Set your timer on a daily basis, ask for help if necessary and get to it!

Wanting to learn Italian at last?
Open a savings account earmarked "Trip to Italy." Put ten dollars in it as a talisman of the fact that the savings

will happen (ten dollars a day perhaps?). Set a date for the future trip. The minute you can afford it, buy your airline tickets. Make yourself accountable to the vision of joy and accomplishment that you hold so dear. Get going on learning that language!

A Reason for Completion is more than a designated deadline. It is a time frame that exists outside of yourself and can include both your finances and other friends. Use these facts to galvanizing effect!

Act as if what you do makes a difference.
It does.

– William James

Reward Yourself

If you really need an incentive, offer yourself a reward
for the completion of whatever it is you seek to create or
conquer. Make the reward something you really want -
perhaps something you have wanted for a long time. Create
a contract with yourself that when you complete your task,
you will get your reward. If necessary, tell your spouse or
a friend and ask them to hold you true to this contract. No
niggling.

Ten Times Three

In the course of writing this book, I often found myself
needing to attack several tasks or goals in a day, in addition
to doing my writing.

For this dilemma, I simply multiplied the theory times three
– making sure that I spent ten minutes a day on the book,
then offering the same time to the other things in my life
that I was creating/conquering (learning Spanish/writing a
will).

Everything got done in a weave of time and engagement
rather than focusing on one aspect at the expense of the
others. The timer helped me here. I listened, and when
it felt right, I knocked off at what I was doing. At other
moments, if the Time Bloom effect had occured, I let

myself stay with my task and simply dug in for as long as I had.

Consider adopting this method if you are needing to create or conquer a number of things. Every day is different, indeed every day you are different, so let the weave of experiences vary. Move with what moves you. You will be amazed at how things will happen.

A word of caution: I don't recommend multi-tasking here, as it will dilute your focus. Let each ten minute time period be about what it is about. As Confucious says : "S/he who chases two rabbits at once, catches neither." You want to catch that rabbit!

Things don't have to be hard to be possible. They also don't have to be hard to be worthy.

Remember the mantra:

Make it easy.

Take it easy.

Keep it easy.

Go!

Divide and Conquer

This approach works when you have a large task that you dread (i.e. cleaning out a sopping, moldy basement after a flood) and you actually have an enough time but your dread is stopping you in your tracks.

Use time in Ten Minute batches. Keep your kitchen timer at the ready and make sure that you have a big thing or several big things that you love doing at the ready. Dive into the dreaded task for ten minutes only and then follow those ten minutes with at least twenty minutes of something you really love to do. Watch a movie. Cook. Dance. Download some new music onto your MP3 player. Read the copy of last Sunday's paper.

Bear in mind that diving into the dreaded task may in fact hook your energies and then the Time Bloom effect will occur. That's okay. You can batch and shape the time any way you want. Just give yourself the rhythm of doing the dreaded thing followed by doing the loved thing. Over and over. It may take much longer for the dreaded task to be completed but who cares? There's no time limit on these things.

The Divide and Conquer method was never more important for me than recently, when I had to amend and resubmit my taxes due to an audit. Doing my taxes once is enough to get my knickers in a twist, but to have to re-do them was literally more than I could bear. So, I engaged the Divide and Conquer method and took breaks, took walks, read magazines and even worked on this book. It helped me keep a balanced frame of mind and peeled off the layers of stress as they were appearing. I even did a better job at the taxes because my stress level was lower when I returned to face the numbers. Most happily, the job got done without me being a wreck at the end. It was a tremendous relief.

Make it Easy and Keep it Fun.

Dive in!

Know When to Pause

In any endeavor, there is a rhythm of energy that keeps the progress flowing forward. Remember that this rhythm often necessitates time to stop, rest, or do something else, as a way of keeping going.

Know yourself and your tendencies.

Take a break if you need to, and then return to your commitment.

If you are having trouble getting back to things, reread the "Words of Advice" sections of the book, and gather what you need...

A buddy.

A reason for completion.

A reward.

Above all else, recognize that pausing can be a crucial strategy for success on the whole, and don't beat yourself up for stepping away from things for awhile.

Take it easy.

When You Have Too Much Time

The old adage "Need to get something done? Ask a busy person," is true. Busy people are in the flow of things. They are engaged, active and productive.

People with too much time on their hands tend to be the opposite. I have experienced this myself, at various points in my life. My sense of initiative went down the drain if I was awash in time. Procrastination became my mode of being. Nothing got done efficiently – indeed, very little got done at all because I could always put things off until the next moment, as there was always the next moment.

The Ten Minute way can help here. If you are stuck, try working at something you need to do for ten minutes a day. More than creating or conquering a task, the method will help you find your way back to your own sense of momentum. If you are really stuck, find a buddy and make yourself accountable to someone else.

Day by day, step by step and action by action you will find your way back to the part of you that makes things happen. The joy in experiencing your accomplishments will spur you on. All you have to do is gently hoist yourself into those first ten minutes, for those first few days.

It will happen. Things will shift.

Begin!

When You Absolutely, Positively Have No Time

Turn off your computer.

As the saying goes: one thing you can't recycle is wasted time. It is ironic how many people are mindful of physical waste and then completely mindless about pouring hours down the drain at a computer. Want to get nothing done? Hang around on the computer for no good reason.

If you can feel that you are about to fall into this abyss, simply look at the clock on your device and give yourself ten minutes. You don't have to go cold turkey and skip the whole juicy thing, just give yourself that time, enjoy what you are doing and when ten minutes passes, be done with it.

Your time is both precious and your own.

Remember to use it well.

Beware of Naysayers

Nothing like a positive step in the new direction to bring out the naysayers everywhere. People who are entrenched in their own inertia often loathe the sight of someone stepping bravely forward into a new, productive place.

Alas, these problem huggers are everywhere.

There is only one approach that works with regard to these people - ignore them completely and let your results speak for themselves.

Go back to considering what you want to create or conquer and set a timer.

Reach for your friends. Trust yourself.

Start today.

Nothing splendid has ever been achieved
except by those who dared to believe
that something inside them was superior to
circumstance.

– Bruce Barton, Author, Politician

6

Specific Ideas

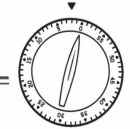

You and Your Physical Wellness

Fitness is not just a fad. To be well in ourselves and well in our world, we need to be in some kind of decent shape. While a trip to the gym, a serious hike or a ten mile bike ride is sublime, often finding time to be in daily motion can be a daunting task. For people who work full time jobs, the challenge of staying fit can sometimes feel impossible.

Recent research has taught us that frequent exercise, even if done for short periods of time, is far more beneficial that the occasional huge blast of exertion. Ten minutes a day of walking, running or yoga can significantly change how you feel in your body and thus how you feel in your world. Remember the math – ten minutes a day is seventy minutes a week. That's a lot of exercise to get or to miss.

Consider these ideas:

Leave your office and walk for ten minutes before you sit down for lunch. Walk five minutes out and five minutes back. If it's raining, walk around your office or up and down some stairs.

At home, wear clothes that are easy to move in and then do ten minutes of yoga without changing. Simply grab your mat and begin. Or forget the mat and do standing postures. The breathing alone will revitalize you.

Put on your favorite music and close your eyes and dance. If you close your eyes, then even you won't be watching and you can really get a groove on.

Leave hand weights in a place where they are easy to retrieve. Define a simple workout for yourself, set a timer and go for it.

Follow the age old adage that you should never take an elevator if you can take the stairs.

Remember, keep it easy to create. You are more likely to exercise if it is convenient. And physical activity doesn't require a change of clothes or a specific place. You go out dancing wearing regular clothing, right?

There is a host of efficient ideas available out there. There are many structured programs available and even apps you can download to your smartphone. A quick, yes, ten minute search on the internet will inspire you.

The only thing you really need is your own desire.

Start today.

Your Emotional Wellness
Ten Minutes to Connect

I have a friend who thinks that social media sites have ruined relationships. "You log on, post something and think you've actually connected with people....but you really haven't."

While I am sure there are a multitude of responses to this comment, I think she has a point. As contacting people has become easier than ever, true connection seems to have become more elusive.

In terms of communication, I think there is nothing more powerful than actually looking someone in the eye. If that is not possible, calling someone, even briefly, can convey your presence.

It's easy to think that you can't call or see someone because you don't have a lot of time. In truth, connecting can take only a handful of minutes.

Think about your life and consider who you want to be in touch with.

How can you use a small amount of time, today, to reach them in a meaningful way?

How can you use ten minutes today to reconnect with -

your partner/your spouse
your children
your friends

your extended family
your neighbors

One idea is to get together for a brief time with no agenda.
No plan whatsoever, except to be together. In today's super
busy world, even the idea of this can seem like nonsense.
But in these moments where there is no expectation of time,
experience or one another, great things can happen.

We don't know the value of what we do until we do it.

– Tama Kieves,
Career Change /Transition Coach

You and Your Spiritual Wellness
Ten Minutes OFF

This is a brief, complete vacation.

Recess: grown up style.

Do nothing.

Sit down or lie down and rest.

Set a timer (or don't even bother) and as you begin, check in with yourself. Imagine that you gather up all your heavy thoughts and responsibilities, put them in a brown paper bag and leave them outside the door.

Be sure to close the door.

Scan your body and make a gentle, mental note of how you are feeling

both physically and emotionally.

Don't judge or change anything.

Just notice.

The first time you do this, you may feel wildly restless. That's okay. Just notice.

Remind yourself that the bag with all your responsibilities is beyond your reach.

Stay with it and when your timer goes off, take note of how you feel.

Different than when you started?

Probably.

This is a process where the cumulative effects are really evident.

The first few days you do it, you may wonder why you are bothering.

But soon thereafter, you may find a new sense of calm emerging from within

and your whole system looking forward to the quiet.

Remember -

Doing nothing is in fact doing something.

Take time to be still.

Your system will relish the rest.

Ten Minutes ANYTIME

Simply sit or stand where you are and breathe soft, complete breaths.

For ten minutes.

Don't worry about emptying your mind, repeating a mantra or changing how you feel.

Simply breathe.

You can do this sitting in your car before you go into the house at the end of the day.

You can do this standing in a crowded subway as you make your way to work.

You can do it as you wait in a long line to get to the checkout counter.

You can do it in a bathroom stall at the office, at the grocery store, at school or anywhere.

You can do it right now.

This act alone, practiced every day will bring a change within you.

And as within, without.

Make it easy. Take it easy. Keep it easy.

Breathe.

Ten Minutes of Radical
Self Acceptance

A few years ago, I took a trip to the Orkney Islands, off the northern coast of Scotland. The environment there shocked me, but not in the way I expected. It was not at all the barren, wet sheepy place that had lurked in my imaginings.

Instead, I found a sleek, informal elegance everywhere. Every inch of the environment was lovingly cared for in a way that seemed inherently wholesome. Every fence was mended, every pillar painted, the lambs seemed happy and visitors seemed to be truly welcome. It was the only place I've ever been to where the environment itself seemed to have complete self-esteem.

Inspired by this, I decided to expand my vacation to my inner world. I took a total break from self-criticism and self-doubt. Every time I could feel some kind of niggling, devil-thought emerge, I would pause, breathe and gently release it. I was on vacation. From everything.

The relief was tremendous, particularly when I would see myself in a mirror or catch my reflection in a shop window. Gone was the rapid fire "maybe you should... bla-di-bla-bla." What arose instead was a sense of simple, complete calm. And an okayness with what was.

The experience was both profound and unforgettable. I wish I could say I have lived that way ever since. I haven't but at least I know what it's like to live that way for awhile.

Consider spending ten minutes a day, today, on vacation

from your inner critic. In your mind, take that critic by the hand and gently walk it to the door. Usher it outside and close the door.

Notice how you feel.

You don't have to worry about welcoming it back. Inner critics have a way of showing up by themselves, whether they're welcome or not.

Therefore, repeat when needed or desired.

House Zap

I used to know a woman in London who never used the word "clean" about that action one is supposed to do around the house. She would use the word "zap" and simply say: "It's time to zap the house!"

It was a galvanizing thing to hear and a dynamic invitation - the opposite of drudge!

In her honor are two ideas for Ten Minute House Zaps...

Zap One – Ten Minutes Before Bed

These days people are so busy, it's hard to even find the energy to brush your teeth at bedtime. But it's really worth it to spend ten minutes at night to organize your living space. This falls into the "conquer" category because who wants to spend ten minutes doing that?

Think of it as a gift you are giving yourself the following morning. It may feel like nothing if you go to bed with your house in a tip. But it will feel awful to wake up and find it that way. Especially if you are tired in the morning

Even the simplest bit of sorting can have a huge impact on how you experience your living space. And as everyone knows, a de-cluttered space represents a de-cluttered mind. Waking up to a home in order sets a tone for the whole day. You're organized which means you are ready to go.

If it seems like too big a task, then create order in the places you are likely to be in the morning. The places that will first hit your eyes, after you get out of bed. The hallway? The living room? The kitchen? (Yes, probably the kitchen.) Order those places and if you're too tired to do them all, do one a night.

Test this theory for yourself. Try it out and see if you don't feel better experiencing your surroundings when they are in a sense of order.

Zap Two – After the Party

We already know there is nothing worse than waking up the day after a fabulous party you've hosted and finding yourself exhausted, possibly hungover and facing a house that looks like a tornado hit it.

Protect yourself from this horror by doing a Ten Minute House Zap before bed.

Here's what to do:

No matter how tired you are at the end of the night, set the timer and take Ten Minutes to attack the situation by batching and piling. Cocktail napkins scrunched up all over the living room floor? Put them all in a pile. Ditto the plates. Gather all the glasses into one area and do the same for the silverware. Follow this idea with dining table chaos as well.

Briefly put the furniture back together if pillows and seat cushions have become uprooted or the furniture itself has gotten pushed around.

Is there more than one of you? Assign one person to a room. A lot can get done!

Wipe down the sinks in the bathroom and kitchen.

Take stock when your timer goes off and look all around. Remember that this is what the tired you of tomorrow will see. Looks good? Great. Go to bed.

Remember, you are not cleaning up per se, you are giving yourself the gift of waking up to a house that has a sense of visual order and has been prepared to be cleaned. This, in turn, will make cleaning easier.

Think of how much better you will feel going to bed the night of the party, knowing you have done this for yourself. Think of how much better you will feel tomorrow morning.

Try it.

You and Your Kids

As any parent knows, having kids = having clutter.

Use the MAKE IT HAPPEN method with your kitchen timer to turn cleaning up into a game. Let the timer be the voice of authority. When it rings, the kids are free to stop what they are doing, no matter how much or how little they have accomplished.

The timer will often work to create a game, making kids super efficient.

Some tips:

If the room is really a disaster, assign your child to a section of the room or particular type of toy (e.g. dolls, cars, train pieces). If you have more than one child, likewise divide the instructions.

Truly follow that clock, and allow the timer to be the end of the cleaning requirement. Then, repeat the experience the next day. Continue in daily waves until the room is clean.

Two things to consider:

Children, particularly young children, have a different sense of time. Time is longer to them. It may be necessary to begin with five minutes instead of ten.

It may be necessary to tell your kids that the cleaning that gets done needs to be greater than the mess that gets created, so the room is getting perpetually cleaner, rather than cycling between clean and messy, clean and messy.

Ten Minutes and Your Car

For those of us who drive a lot, and that is many of us, our cars can become extensions of our homes and major holders of all sorts of junk. The car ends up being part unattended trash can, part storage unit, part closet, part post office. We think we are used to it but being around that clutter can be really deadening.

My own challenge is that I never remember to sort/chuck/bring things in from the car until I am actually in the car and at that point, it feels like it's too late to do anything about it. Or is it?

Ten Minutes a Day can be whittled down to Two Minutes a Day to help you here. Each time you get out of your car, grab three pieces of the trash you don't want in there and chuck it in the nearest trash can. Don't pressure yourself to "clean" the car. Just grab three things - each time you leave.

Ditto for all the things that need to be taken back into your home. Don't ask yourself to bring everything in at one time – you probably already have your hands full. Bring one or two things in each time. Your raincoat. That magazine. Your son's tennis racquet. You're car will be clean before you know it and it will actually be more of a pleasure to ride in. You may not think you care but once the space and order has returned, you will feel the difference.

Eventually, you may even get to the point where you only ever have a few things to take out or bring in, and your car will then be in a constant state of orderliness.

Wouldn't that be something?

You and Your Friends
– Gang of Ten Party

Cleaning out the garage? Building a giant igloo for your kids? You name it. With a gang of friends, powerful things can happen in a very short time. Much like an old fashioned barn raising, this is a way of creating a community of people who attack a large task and get it accomplished quickly.

How to Make it Happen

Invite ten spirited and generous friends over. Be sure that everyone understands the nature of the event - you have a big task to create or conquer and need their help in getting it done. Provide great food, good music and a completely relaxed atmosphere.

Once your guests have arrived, introduce the task to everyone and make sure that people have a sense of what is expected of them. Find out if anyone has any limitations (back problems, allergies etc.) and make accommodations when necessary.

Start by having two friends help you for ten minutes with the task. When this first wave of work time is up, have three different friends take over and you and the first two knock off.

Find a way to mark the time that isn't noisily disruptive to the party. Create an easy weave of work and play, so that the transitions won't feel too jarring to your guests.

Stay fluid and go with what seems to be working for the event. Keep it lively and fun. Need more than ten minutes for each work group? Make it happen. Want someone to remain a constant presence at the party to make sure the fun keeps flowing? Choose that lucky person.

Rotate people in and out of the action in natural increments. Keep the emphasis balanced between the party and the task but stay open to the Time Bloom effect and acknowledge that some people won't want to stop working and perhaps someone won't want to leave the party!

Figure out how it will work best for you as host of the event and don't forget that the "party" part applies to you too. Take time to enjoy yourself even though you are in charge.

Once the task is complete, gather everyone for an "after party" (the best part of any party, in my opinion) where everyone kicks backs, feels proud and relishes the great accomplishments of the day.

Then prepare yourself to be invited to similar events at the homes of the people who helped you. The day's accomplishments will be striking and will undoubtedly serve as inspiration to everyone involved.

Remember, people love to help.

Let them.

Planning

For people who lead busy multi-dimensional lives, the time it takes to plan those lives takes serious consideration. It is easy to ignore this fact or to wish it away. But if you take a handful of minutes and line up how your next fews days or weeks will unfold, you may find they unfold with more ease.

Look at planning as part of how your care for your life. It is you working on your life as opposed to you working at your life. Good planning can offer up clarity – if you know how and when activities will unfold, you can relax in knowing what is coming next.

We all know that life offers up its share of curveballs – some small, some gigantic. We have no control over those moments. But we can control much of the flow of our daily time and activities in a way that gives us a sense of ease in knowing what's to come.

As a great lover of spontaneity and going with the flow, I resisted the idea of planning for years. I was sure I would feel restricted by knowing what was clearly to come. I was both shocked and surprised to learn that planning somehow gave me more time to be spontaneous. Because I could anticipate much of what was to come, I felt freer in the moments that were undefined.

Can you take ten minutes now and plan the rest of your week? See what it feels like and then notice what unfolds.

7

Some Last Good Words

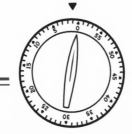

Sweet True Stories

While I was writing this book, my friends and family became inspired to adopt the Ten Minute a Day method in their own lives.

Here's a list of the wonderful things they accomplished:

- My goddaughter began to learn Japanese in preparation for her first trip there.

- My sister finally cleaned out her storage locker and was able to create beautiful repainted furniture for her home.

- My neighbor wrote songs.

- My friend prepared for an important exam at a very overwhelming time in her life.

- Another friend gathered the strength of two pals, completely cleaned out a small building on her property and with her newfound verve, committed herself to conquering the task of clearing out her porch and creating the joy of getting all her family photos presented beautifully around her house.

- Nicole Zaccaria, one of the artists for this book, implemented the Theory of Structured Procrastination to paint the woodwork in her house, and then completed a hideously boring computer task.

Finally

To pick up this book, read it, smile and do nothing would be like buying a postcard of the Grand Canyon and thinking you had actually seen the place. Or as the brilliant internet marketing guru Perry Marshall would say, an "Adventure in Missing the Point."

To Make it Happen, you need to dive in. Remember, you are only ever asking for ten minutes of yourself. We throw away whole groups of ten minutes every day without even noticing. Recapture this handful of time, and on a daily basis, commit to it.

Unlike many self-help ideas, this is not a McQuickly solution. This is a gentle, measured method for making your life happen. Intention is everything, and your intention is always your own to direct.

Try the ten minute plan for seven days at first. Chart your progress and your feelings. You don't have to write it down, but make an internal note to yourself, or tell your buddy, your partner, or someone, what you have noticed after seven days. I guarantee you will notice something. At the very least, I suspect you will find yourself in new mode of doing.

As the book ends, so may you begin. For support and continued inspiration, join the MAKE IT HAPPEN online community in the various social media forums listed in the Online Resources.

Online Resources

Friend us on Facebook.

Follow us on Twitter.

Point to us on Pinterest.

www.makeithappenintenminutesaday.com

Acknowledgements

First and foremost, let me thank Blair Benjamin, Creator and Director of the remarkable program Assets for Artists. I have been privileged to be a part of the Assets program and while at a meeting in 2010, I had the chance to talk about discovering the MAKE IT HAPPEN method. "There's a book!" Blair exclaimed. How right he was. Without his idea and enthusiasm, this book would not be here. Thank you, Blair.

I thank my astonishing co-creators: Designers of the book and website, Danny and Ulana Chapman; Artists Michelle Raczkowski and Nicole Zaccaria; language specialist Dana Katz and brilliant wordsmith, Emily Rechnitz. Each of these amazing individuals gave generously of their time and talent and this book would not be what it is without them.

A special note of thanks to Emily DeVoti, amazing playwright and extraordinary friend, for alerting me early on to the importance of using images. It is thanks to Emily that this book is fun to look at as well as fun to read.

On the business side of things, my thanks to Esther Robinson for being a bomb of inspiration about the financial realities of a creative life. Additionally, I received great advice from the team at the Small Business Development Center of Western MA: Keith Girouard, Nancy Shulman and Andrea Morris. Thanks to all.

Further business inspiration was offered to me from people who didn't even know they helped: John Assaraf, Vic Johnson, Perry Marshall and Bob Procter.

I am deeply grateful to my many loving friends who offered support and ideas along the way: Shelley Babicka, Barney Bardsley, Lorimer Burns, Sari Cohen, Emily Hall, Karen Greco, Jennifer Kenny, Lisa Kors, Emily Paskus, Brian Savelson, Toni Small, Fin Walker, Ann Zaccaria and Alida and Sarah Zimmerman.

And finally my thanks to DD, MA, Kook, Henry and most of all to Shugie, who inspires me to get up and MAKE IT HAPPEN every day.

Create

Conquer

Where I Am Now

Where I Want to Be

Time Frame

I hear and I forget.
I see and I remember.
I do and I understand.

– Confucius

Lorne Holden is an award winning artist
and author living in New England.